HUNTSMAN, WHAT QUARRY?

Huntsman, What Quarry?

POEMS BY
EDNA ST. VINCENT MILLAY

HARPER & BROTHERS *Publishers*
New York *and* London
MCMXXXIX

HUNTSMAN, WHAT QUARRY?

5-9

FIRST EDITION
D-O

To

Llewelyn Powys and Alyse Gregory

CONTENTS

PART ONE

viii

PART ONE

THE BALLAD OF CHALDON DOWN

In April, when the yellow whin
Was out of doors, and I within,—
And magpies nested in the thorn
Where not a man of woman born
Might spy upon them, save he be
Content to bide indefinitely
On Chaldon Heath, hung from a pin,
A great man in a small thorn tree—

In April, when, as I have said,
The golden gorse was all in bloom,
And I confinèd to my room,
And there confinèd to my bed,
As sick as mortal man could be,
A lady came from over the sea,
All for to say good-day to me.

All in a green and silver gown,
With half its flounces in her hand,
She came across the windy down,
She came, and pricked the furrowed land
With heels of slippers built for town,
All for to say good-day to me.

The Channel fog was in her hair,
Her cheek was cool with Channel fog.
Pale cowslips from the sloping hedge,
And samphire from the salty ledge,
And the sweet myrtle of the bog
She brought me as I languished there;
But of the blackthorn, the blue sloe,
No branch to lay a body low.

She came to me by ditch and stile,
She came to me through heather and brake,
And many and many a flinty mile
She walked in April for my sake,
All for to say good-day to me.

She came by way of Lulworth Cove,
She came by way of Diffey's Farm;
All in a green and silver frock,
With half its flounces over her arm,
By the Bat's Head at dusk she came,
Where inland from the Channel drove
The fog, and from the Shambles heard
The horn above the hidden rock;

And startled many a wild sea-bird
To fly unseen from Durdle Door
Into the fog; and left the shore,
And found a track without a name
That led to Chaldon, and so came
Over the downs to Chydyok,
All for to say good-day to me.

All for to ask me only this—
As she shook out her skirts to dry,
And laughed, and looked me in the eye,
And gave me two cold hands to kiss:
That I be steadfast, that I lie
And strengthen and forbear to die.
All for to say that I must be
Son of my sires, who lived to see
The gorse in bloom at ninety-three,
All for to say good-day to me.

INERT PERFECTION

"INERT Perfection, let me chip your shell.
You cannot break it through with that soft beak.
What if you broke it never, and it befell
You should not issue thence, should never speak?"

Perfection in the egg, a fluid thing,
Grows solid in due course, and there exists;
Knowing no urge to struggle forth and sing;
Complete, though shell-bound. But the mind insists

It shall be hatched . . . to this ulterior end:
That it be bound by Function, that it be
Less than Perfection, having to expend
Some force on a nostalgia to be free.

SONG FOR YOUNG LOVERS IN A CITY

Though less for love than for the deep
Though transient death that follows it
These childish mouths grown soft in sleep
Here in a rented bed have met,

They have not met in love's despite . . .
Such tiny loves will leap and flare
Lurid as coke-fires in the night,
Against a background of despair.

To treeless grove, to grey retreat
Descend in flocks from corniced eaves
The pigeons now on sooty feet,
To cover them with linden leaves.

THANKSGIVING DINNER

AH, BROKEN garden, frost on the melons and on the
    beans!
Frozen are the ripe tomatoes, the red fruit and the
    hairy golden stem;
Frozen are the grapes, and the vine above them
    frozen, and the peppers are frozen!
And I walk among them smiling,—for what of them?

I can live on the woody fibres of the overgrown
Kohl-rabi, on the spongy radish coarse and hot,
I can live on what the squirrels may have left of the
    beechnuts and the acorns . . .
For pride in my love, who might well have died,
    and did not.

I will cook for my love a banquet of beets and cab-
    bages,
Leeks, potatoes, turnips, all such fruits . . .
For my clever love, who has returned from further
    than the far east;
We will laugh like spring above the steaming, stolid
    winter roots.

THE SNOW STORM

No HAWK hangs over in this air:
The urgent snow is everywhere.
The wing adroiter than a sail
Must lean away from such a gale,
Abandoning its straight intent,
Or else expose tough ligament
And tender flesh to what before
Meant dampened feathers, nothing more.

Forceless upon our backs there fall
Infrequent flakes hexagonal,
Devised in many a curious style
To charm our safety for a while,
Where close to earth like mice we go
Under the horizontal snow.

ENGLISH SPARROWS

(Washington Square)

How sweet the sound in the city an hour before
 sunrise,
When the park is empty and grey and the light clear
 and so lovely
I must sit on the floor before my open window for
 an hour with my arms on the sill
And my cheek on my arm, watching the spring sky's
Soft suffusion from the roofed horizon upward with
 palest rose,
Doting on the charming sight with eyes
Open, eyes closed;
Breathing with quiet pleasure the cool air cleansed
 by the night, lacking all will
To let such happiness go, nor thinking the least
 thing ill
In me for such indulgence, pleased with the day and
 with myself. How sweet
The noisy chirping of the urchin sparrows from crev-
 ice and shelf
Under my window, and from down there in the
 street,
Announcing the advance of the roaring competitive
 day with city bird-song.

A bumbling bus
Goes under the arch. A man bareheaded and alone
Walks to a bench and sits down.
He breathes the morning with me; his thoughts are
    his own.
Together we watch the first magnanimous
Rays of the sun on the tops of greening trees and
    on houses of red brick and of stone.

MORTAL FLESH, IS NOT YOUR PLACE IN THE GROUND?

MORTAL flesh, is not your place in the ground?—
    Why do you stare so
At the bright planet serene in the clear green evening
    sky above the many-coloured streakèd clouds?—
Your brows drawn together as if to chide, your
    mouth set as if in anger.

Learn to love blackness while there is yet time,
    blackness
Unpatterned, blackness without horizons.

Beautiful are the trees in autumn, the emerald pines
Dark among the light-red leaves of the maple and
    the dark-red
Leaves of the white oak and the indigo long
Leaves of the white ash.
But why do you stand so, staring with stern face of
    ecstasy at the autumn leaves,
At the boughs hung with banners along the road as
    if a procession were about to pass?

Learn to love roots instead, that soon above your
    head shall be as branches.

IMPRESSION: FOG OFF THE COAST OF DORSET

As DAY was born, as night was dying,
The seagulls woke me with their crying;
And from the reef the mooing horn
Spoke to the waker: Day is born
And night is dying, but still the fog
On dimly looming deck and spar
Is dewy, and on the vessel's log,
And cold the first-mate's fingers are,
And wet the pen wherewith they write
"Off Portland. Fog. No land in sight."
—As night was dying, and glad to die,
And day, with dull and gloomy eye,
Lifting the sun, a smoky lamp,
Peered into fog, that swaddled sky
And wave alike: a shifty damp
Unwieldy province, loosely ruled,
Turned over to a prince unschooled,
That he must govern with sure hand
Straightway, not knowing sea from land.

THE RABBIT

Hearing the hawk squeal in the high sky
I and the rabbit trembled.
Only the dark small rabbits newly kittled in their
    neatly dissembled
Hollowed nest in the thicket thatched with straw
Did not respect his cry.
At least, not that I saw.

But I have said to the rabbit with rage and a hun-
    dred times, "Hop!
Streak it for the bushes! Why do you sit so still?
You are bigger than a house, I tell you, you are big-
    ger than a hill, you are a beacon for air-planes!
O indiscreet!
And the hawk and all my friends are out to kill!
Get under cover!" But the rabbit never stirred; she
    never will.

And I shall see again and again the large eye blaze
With death, and gently glaze;
The leap into the air I shall see again and again, and
    the kicking feet;
And the sudden quiet everlasting, and the blade of
    grass green in the strange mouth of the inter-
    rupted grazer.

TRUCE FOR A MOMENT

TRUCE for a moment between Earth and Ether
Slackens the mind's allegiance to despair:
Shyly confer earth, water, fire and air
With the fifth essence.

For the duration, if the mind require it,
Trigged is the wheel of Time against the slope;
Infinite Space lies curved within the scope
Of the hand's cradle.

Thus between day and evening in the autumn,
High in the west alone and burning bright,
Venus has hung, the earliest riding-light
In the calm harbour.

NOT SO FAR AS THE FOREST

I

THAT chill is in the air
Which the wise know well, and even have learned
    to bear.
This joy, I know,
Will soon be under snow.

The sun sets in a cloud
And is not seen.
Beauty, that spoke aloud,
Addresses now only the remembering ear.
The heart begins here
To feed on what has been.

Night falls fast.
Today is in the past.

Blown from the dark hill hither to my door
Three flakes, then four
Arrive, then many more.

II

BRANCH by branch
This tree has died. Green only
Is one last bough, moving its leaves in the sun.

What evil ate its root, what blight,
What ugly thing,
Let the mole say, the bird sing;
Or the white worm behind the shedding bark
Tick in the dark.

You and I have only one thing to do:
Saw the trunk through.

III

Distressèd mind, forbear
To tease the hooded Why;
That shape will not reply.

From the warm chair
To the wind's welter
Flee, if storm's your shelter.

But no, you needs must part,
Fling him his release—
On whose ungenerous heart
Alone you are at peace.

IV

Not dead of wounds, not borne
Home to the village on a litter of branches, torn
By splendid claws and the talk all night of the vil-
  lagers,
But stung to death by gnats
Lies Love.

What swamp I sweated through for all these years
Is at length plain to me.

V

Poor passionate thing,
Even with this clipped wing how well you flew!—
   though not so far as the forest.

Unwounded and unspent, serene but for the eye's
   bright trouble,
Was it the lurching flight, the unequal wind under
   the lopped feathers that brought you down,
To sit in folded colours on the level empty field,
Visible as a ship, paling the yellow stubble?

Rebellious bird, warm body foreign and bright,
Has no one told you?—Hopeless is your flight
Towards the high branches. Here is your home,
Between the barnyard strewn with grain and the
   forest tree.
Though Time refeather the wing,
Ankle slip the ring,
The once-confinèd thing
Is never again free.

RENDEZVOUS

Not for these lovely blooms that prank your cham-
bers did I come. Indeed,
I could have loved you better in the dark;
That is to say, in rooms less bright with roses,
rooms more casual, less aware
Of History in the wings about to enter with benev-
olent air
On ponderous tiptoe, at the cue "Proceed."
Not that I like the ash-trays over-crowded and the
place in a mess,
Or the monastic cubicle too unctuously austere and
stark,
But partly that these formal garlands for our Eighth
Street Aphrodite are a bit too Greek,
And partly that to make the poor walls rich with
our unaided loveliness
Would have been more *chic.*

Yet here I am, having told you of my quarrel with
the taxi-driver over a line of Milton, and you
laugh; and you are you, none other.
Your laughter pelts my skin with small delicious
blows.
But I am perverse: I wish you had not scrubbed—
with pumice, I suppose—
The tobacco stains from your beautiful fingers. And
I wish I did not feel like your mother.

MODERN DECLARATION

I, HAVING loved ever since I was a child a few things, never having wavered
In these affections; never through shyness in the houses of the rich or in the presence of clergymen having denied these loves;
Never when worked upon by cynics like chiropractors having grunted or clicked a vertebra to the discredit of these loves;
Never when anxious to land a job having diminished them by a conniving smile; or when befuddled by drink
Jeered at them through heartache or lazily fondled the fingers of their alert enemies; declare

That I shall love you always.
No matter what party is in power;
No matter what temporarily expedient combination of allied interests wins the war;
Shall love you always.

THE FITTING

THE fitter said, "*Madame, vous avez maigri,*"
And pinched together a handful of skirt at my hip.
"*Tant mieux,*" I said, and looked away slowly, and
took my under-lip
Softly between my teeth.

Rip—rip!
Out came the seam, and was pinned together in another place.
She knelt before me, a hardworking woman with a
familiar and unknown face,
Dressed in linty black, very tight in the arm's-eye
and smelling of sweat.
She rose, lifting my arm, and set her cold shears
against me,—snip-snip;
Her knuckles gouged my breast. My drooped eyes
lifted to my guarded eyes in the glass, and
glanced away as from someone they had never
met.

"*Ah, que madame a maigri!*" cried the *vendeuse,*
coming in with dresses over her arm.
"*C'est la chaleur,*" I said, looking out into the sunny
tops of the horse-chestnuts—and indeed it was
very warm.

I stood for a long time so, looking out into the afternoon, thinking of the evening and you. . . .

While they murmured busily in the distance, turning me, touching my secret body, doing what
they were paid to do.

INTENTION TO ESCAPE FROM HIM

I THINK I will learn some beautiful language, useless
   for commercial
Purposes, work hard at that.
I think I will learn the Latin name of every song-
   bird, not only in America but wherever they
   sing.
(Shun meditation, though; invite the controversial:
Is the world flat? Do bats eat cats?) By digging
   hard I might deflect that river, my mind, that
   uncontrollable thing,
Turgid and yellow, strong to overflow its banks in
   spring, carrying away bridges;
A bed of pebbles now, through which there trickles
   one clear narrow stream, following a course
   henceforth nefast—

Dig, dig; and if I come to ledges, blast.

WHAT SAVAGE BLOSSOM

Do I not know what savage blossom only under the
    pitting hail
Of your inclement season could have prospered?
    Here lie
Green leaves to wade in, and of the many roads not
    one road leading outward from this place
But is blocked by boughs that will hiss and simmer
    when they burn—green autumn, lady, green
    autumn on this land!

Do I not know what inward pressure only could in-
    flate its petals to withstand
(No, no, not hate, not hate) the onslaught of a little
    time with you?

No, no, not love, not love. Call it by name,
Now that it's over, now that it is gone and cannot
    hear us.

It was an honest thing. Not noble. Yet no shame.

THE ROAD TO THE PAST

IT IS this that you get for being so far-sighted. Not
    so many years
For the myopic, as for me,
The delightful shape, implored and hard of heart,
    proceeding
Into the past unheeding,
(No wave of the hand, no backward look to see
If I still stand there) clear and precise along that
    road appears.

The trees that edge that road run parallel
For eyes like mine past many towns, past hell seen
    plainly;
All that has happened shades that street;
Children all day, even the awkward, the ungainly
Of mind, work out on paper problems more abstruse;
Demonstrably these eyes will close
Before those hedges meet.

"FONTAINE, JE NE BOIRAI PAS DE TON EAU!"

I KNOW I might have lived in such a way
As to have suffered only pain:
Loving not man nor dog;
Not money, even; feeling
Toothache perhaps, but never more than an hour
    away
From skill and novocaine;
Making no contacts, dealing with life through
    agents, drinking one cocktail, betting two dol-
    lars, wearing raincoats in the rain;
Betrayed at length by no one but the fog
Whispering to the wing of the plane.

"Fountain," I have cried to that unbubbling well,
    "I will not drink of thy water!" Yet I thirst
For a mouthful of—not to swallow, only to rinse my
    mouth in—peace. And while the eyes of the
    past condemn,
The eyes of the present narrow into assignation.
    And . . . worst . . .
The young are so old, they are born with their fin-
    gers crossed; I shall get no help from them.

THE PLAID DRESS

STRONG sun, that bleach
The curtains of my room, can you not render
Colourless this dress I wear?—
This violent plaid
Of purple angers and red shames; the yellow stripe
Of thin but valid treacheries; the flashy green of kind
    deeds done
Through indolence, high judgments given in haste;
The recurring checker of the serious breach of taste?

No more uncoloured than unmade,
I fear, can be this garment that I may not doff;
Confession does not strip it off,
To send me homeward eased and bare;

All through the formal, unoffending evening, under
    the clean
Bright hair,
Lining the subtle gown . . . it is not seen,
But it is there.

THE TRUE ENCOUNTER

"Wolf!" cried my cunning heart
    At every sheep it spied,
    And roused the countryside.

"Wolf! Wolf!"—and up would start
    Good neighbours, bringing spade
    And pitchfork to my aid.

At length my cry was known:
    Therein lay my release.
I met the wolf alone
    And was devoured in peace.

PART TWO

CZECHO-SLOVAKIA

IF THERE were balm in Gilead, I would go
To Gilead for your wounds, unhappy land,
Gather you balsam there, and with this hand,
Made deft by pity, cleanse and bind and sew
And drench with healing, that your strength might
    grow,
(Though love be outlawed, kindness contraband)
And you, O proud and felled, again might stand;
But where to look for balm, I do not know.
The oils and herbs of mercy are so few;
Honour's for sale; allegiance has its price;
The barking of a fox has bought us all;
We save our skins a craven hour or two.—
While Peter warms him in the servants' hall
The thorns are platted and the cock crows twice.

TWO VOICES

Let us be circumspect, surrounded as we are
By every foe but one, and he from the woods watch-
    ing.
Let us be courteous, since we cannot be wise, guilty
    of no neglect, pallid with seemly terror, yet re-
    garding with indulgent eyes
Violence, and compromise.

SECOND VOICE

We shall learn nothing; or we shall learn it too late.
    Why should we wait
For Death, who knows the road so well? Need we
    sit hatching—
Such quiet fowl as we, meek to the touch,—a clutch
    of adder's eggs? Let us not turn them; let us
    not keep them warm; let us leave our nests and
    flock and tell
All that we know, all that we can piece together, of
    a time when all went, or seemed to go, well.

SAY THAT WE SAW SPAIN DIE

SAY that we saw Spain die. O splendid bull, how
   well you fought!
Lost from the first.
               . . . the tossed, the replaced, the
   watchful *torero* with gesture elegant and spry,
Before the dark, the tiring but the unglazed eye de-
   ploying the bright cape,
Which hid for once not air, but the enemy indeed,
   the authentic shape,
A thousand of him, interminably into the ring re-
   leased . . . the turning beast at length between
   converging colours caught.

Save for the weapons of its skull, a bull
Unarmed, considering, weighing, charging
Almost a world, itself without ally.

Say that we saw the shoulders more than the mind
   confused, so profusely
Bleeding from so many more than the accustomed
   barbs, the game gone vulgar, the rules abused.

Say that we saw Spain die from loss of blood, a rustic
   reason, in a reinforced
And proud punctilious land, no *espada*—
A hundred men unhorsed,

A hundred horses gored, and the afternoon aging,
    and the crowd growing restless (all, all so much
    later than planned),
And the big head heavy, sliding forward in the sand,
    and the tongue dry with sand,—no *espada*
Toward that hot neck, for the delicate and final
    thrust, having dared trust forth his hand.

FROM A TOWN IN A STATE OF SIEGE

I

Lie here, and we shall die, but try to take me
Before they come; their droning wings have roared
So close so many times, that I am bored
With death; now give me life instead, now break me
With life, so make me what they could not make me:
Dead, yet myself—this blood, so stingy-stored,
Lavish in death against your body poured—
And if I sleep . . . and if they come . . . then wake me.

Look, I will braid our hair into a braid—
Such lanky locks!—and this is you and me.
The night is very calm: another raid,
I think. I see your mouth—oh, I can see.
No, you have loved me: I am not afraid;
I just was wondering if it would be we.

II

WELL, we have lived so far; we are alive;
War is a way of living. If today
We die, we have to do that anyway
Sometime. It's not so bad, once you contrive
To make a home of it; we do not thrive,
Yet here we are, at least,—no place to stay,
A place to stop in, though—and we can say
Hello to friends; and I have learned to drive.

The worst is being hated, and to hate;
Perhaps if it were hurricane or flood
That dragged us from our beds, we might await
The shock, the twisted wreckage and the mud
With lighter hearts, that being not man, but fate . . .
And only friendly dogs to lap our blood.

III

He has no grudge at all, the grievously
Abruptly prematurely newly killed;
To him who cannot smell pine-boards, not-willed
And willed are one: none is so quick as he
To cancel quarrels—let the dead past be
(And the dead future also). Not unskilled
In living are the moment-eaters, filled
With Now,—so might he see it, could he see.

We were attacked—what of it?—we could go
And lie in hiding; we were free to run
From Death!—and this will not again be so.
Now he is free from nothing: man and gun
Have spat into his face; the mouth I know
In memory, sleeps defiled by everyone.

IV

Let me recall his valour, not his love;
Love was his loneliness; his limping pride,
Save when we lay bewildered side by side,
Was on its feet all day; he could not move
Wrong—as most patient history stood to prove—
By dying up against it; but he tried.
The walls are washed, the doors flung open wide,
The city conquered, he not spoken of.

Time does not forfeit; Time does not abstain:
The future in one fist, he eats the past.
I know this; yet again and yet again
I try to hold the present, make it last
One moment, that the simple great be slain
Not unperceived. No hope—Time eats so fast.

V

BUT if you loved me it was long ago
And gurgled with the emptying of the year.
Shall I remember—sitting silent here
Watching the pulsing and the bright outflow
Of vintages we all had come to know
As excellent, seeing without a tear
The future bashed and jetting, bold, not clear—
Love?—and if once you loved me, whether or no?

I forget nothing; every airiest thing
You said, I could recall, or I replied;
I have no time for such remembering:
The world is in an accident, has died
Perhaps already—ambulance! ding-ding!—
Something instructs the corpuscle inside.

THREE SONNETS IN TETRAMETER

I

SEE how these masses mill and swarm
And troop and muster and assail:
God!—We could keep this planet warm
By friction, if the sun should fail.
Mercury, Saturn, Venus, Mars:
If no prow cuts your arid seas,
Then in your weightless air no wars
Explode with such catastrophes
As rock our planet all but loose
From its frayed mooring to the sun.
Law will not sanction such abuse
Forever; when the mischief's done,
Planets, rejoice, on which at night
Rains but the twelve-ton meteorite.

II

His stalk the dark delphinium
Unthorned into the tending hand
Releases . . . yet that hour will come . . .
And must, in such a spiny land.
The silky powdery mignonette
Before these gathering dews are gone
May pierce me—does the rose regret
The day she did her armour on?
In that the foul supplants the fair,
The coarse defeats the twice-refined,
Is food for thought, but not despair:
All will be easier when the mind
To meet the brutal age has grown
An iron cortex of its own.

III

No FURTHER from me than my hand
Is China that I loved so well;
Love does not help to understand
The logic of the bursting shell.
Perfect in dream above me yet
Shines the white cone of Fuji-San;
I wake in fear, and weep and sweat . . .
Weep for Yoshida, for Japan.
Logic alone, all love laid by,
Must calm this crazed and plunging star:
Sorrowful news for such as I,
Who hoped—with men just as they are,
Sinful and loving—to secure
A human peace that might endure.

UNDERGROUND SYSTEM

SET the foot down with distrust upon the crust of
    the world—it is thin.
Moles are at work beneath us; they have tunnelled
    the sub-soil
With separate chambers; which at an appointed
    knock
Could be as one, could intersect and interlock. We
    walk on the skin
Of life. No toil
Of rake or hoe, no lime, no phosphate, no rotation
    of crops, no irrigation of the land,
Will coax the limp and flattened grain to stand
On that bad day, or feed to strength the nibbled
    roots of our nation.

Ease has demoralized us, nearly so; we know
Nothing of the rigours of winter: the house has a
    roof against—the car a top against—the snow.
All will be well, we say; it is a habit, like the rising
    of the sun,
For our country to prosper; who can prevail against
    us? No one.

The house has a roof; but the boards of its floor are
    rotting, and hall upon hall
The moles have built their palace beneath us: we
    have not far to fall.

LINES WRITTEN IN RECAPITULATION

I COULD not bring this splendid world nor any trad-
ing beast
In charge of it, to defer, no, not to give ear, not in
the least
Appearance, to my handsome prophecies, which
here I ponder and put by.

I am left simpler, less encumbered, by the conscious-
ness that I shall by no pebble in my dirty sling
avail
To slay one purple giant four feet high and distribute
arms among his tall attendants, who spit at his
name when spitting on the ground:
They will be found one day
Prone where they fell, or dead sitting—and a pock-
marked wall
Supporting the beautiful back straight as an oak
before it is old.

I have learned to fail. And I have had my say.
Yet shall I sing until my voice crack (this being my
leisure, this my holiday)
That man was a special thing and no commodity, a
thing improper to be sold.

THIS DUSKY FAITH

Why, then, weep not,
Since naught's to weep.

Too wild, too hot
For a dead thing,
Altered and cold,
Are these long tears:
Relinquishing
To the sovereign force
Of the pulling past
What you cannot hold
Is reason's course.

Wherefore, sleep.

Or sleep to the rocking
Rather, of this:
The silver knocking
Of the moon's knuckles
At the door of the night;
Death here becomes
Being, nor truckles
To the sun, assumes
Light as its right.

So, too, this dusky faith
In Man, transcends its death,
Shines out, gains emphasis;
Shorn of the tangled past,
Shows its fine skull at last,
Cold, lovely satellite.

PART THREE

THE PRINCESS RECALLS HER ONE
ADVENTURE

HARD is my pillow
Of down from the duck's breast,
Harsh the linen cover;
I cannot rest.

Fall down, my tears,
Upon the fine hem,
Upon the lonely letters
Of my long name;
Drown the sigh of them.

We stood by the lake
And we neither kissed nor spoke;
We heard how the small waves
Lurched and broke,
And chuckled in the rock.

We spoke and turned away.
We never kissed at all.
Fall down, my tears.
I wish that you might fall
On the road by the lake,
Where my cob went lame,
And I stood with the groom
Till the carriage came.

SHORT STORY

In a fine country, in a sunny country,
Among the hills I knew,
I built a house for the wren that lives in the orchard,
And a house for you.

The house I built for the wren had a round entrance,
Neat and very small;
But the house I built for you had a great doorway,
For a lady proud and tall.

You came from a country where the shrubby sweet
    lavender
Lives the mild winter through;
The lavender died each winter in the garden
Of the house I built for you.

You were troubled and came to me because the
    farmer
Called the autumn "the fall";
You thought that a country where the lavender died
    in the winter
Was not a country at all.

The wrens return each year to the house in the
    orchard;
They have lived, they have seen the world, they
    know what's best
For a wren and his wife; in the handsome house I
    gave them
They build their twiggy nest.

But you, you foolish girl, you have gone home
To a leaky castle across the sea,—
To lie awake in linen smelling of lavender,
And hear the nightingale, and long for me.

TO A CALVINIST IN BALI

You that are sprung of northern stock,
And nothing lavish,—born and bred
With tablets at your foot and head,
And CULPA carven in the rock,

Sense with delight but not with ease
The fragrance of the quinine trees,
The *kembang-spatu's* lolling flame
With solemn envy kin to shame.

Ah, be content!—the scorpion's tail
Atones for much; without avail
Under the sizzling solar pan
Our sleeping servant pulls the fan.

Even in this island richly blest,
Where Beauty walks with naked breast,
Earth is too harsh for Heaven to be
One little hour in jeopardy.

PRETTY LOVE, I MUST OUTLIVE YOU

Pretty Love, I must outlive you;
And my little dog Llewelyn,
Dreaming here with treble whimpers,
Jerking paws and twitching nostrils
On the hearth-rug, will outlive you,
If no trap or shot-gun gets him.

Parrots, tortoises and redwoods
Live a longer life than men do,
Men a longer life than dogs do,
Dogs a longer life than love does.

What a fool I was to take you,
Pretty Love, into my household,
Shape my days and nights to charm you,
Center all my hopes about you,
Knowing well I must outlive you,
If no trap or shot-gun gets me.

TO A YOUNG POET

TIME cannot break the bird's wing from the bird.
Bird and wing together
Go down, one feather.

No thing that ever flew,
Not the lark, not you,
Can die as others do.

NO EARTHLY ENTERPRISE

No EARTHLY enterprise
Will cloud this vision; so beware,
You whom I love, when you are weak, of seeking
    comfort stair by stair
Up here: which leads nowhere.

I am at home—oh, I am safe in bed and well tucked
    in—Despair
Put out the light beside my bed.
I smiled, and closed my eyes.
"Goodnight—goodnight," she said.

But you, you do not like this frosty air.

Cold of the sun's eclipse,
When cocks crow for the first time hopeless, and
    dogs in kennel howl,
Abandoning the richly-stinking bone,
And the star at the edge of the shamed and altered
    sun shivers alone,
And over the pond the bat but not the swallow dips,
And out comes the owl.

MENSES

(He speaks, but to himself, being aware how it is with her)

THINK not I have not heard.
Well-fanged the double word
And well-directed flew.

I felt it. Down my side
Innocent as oil I see the ugly venom slide:
Poison enough to stiffen us both, and all our friends;
But I am not pierced, so there the mischief ends.

There is more to be said; I see it coiling;
The impact will be pain.
Yet coil; yet strike again.
You cannot riddle the stout mail I wove
Long since, of wit and love.

As for my answer . . . stupid in the sun
He lies, his fangs drawn:
I will not war with you.

You know how wild you are. You are willing to be
    turned
To other matters; you would be grateful, even.
You watch me shyly. I (for I have learned
More things than one in our few years together)
Chafe at the churlish wind, the unseasonable
    weather.

"Unseasonable?" you cry, with harsher scorn
Than the theme warrants; "Every year it is the same!
'Unseasonable!' they whine, these stupid peasants!
    —and never since they were born
Have they known a spring less wintry! Lord, the
    shame,
The crying shame of seeing a man no wiser than the
    beasts he feeds—
His skull as empty as a shell!"

("Go to. You are unwell.")

Such is my thought, but such are not my words.

"What is the name," I ask, "of those big birds
With yellow breast and low and heavy flight,
That make such mournful whistling?"
                                    "Meadowlarks,"
You answer primly, not a little cheered.

"Some people shoot them." Suddenly your eyes are
    wet
And your chin trembles. On my breast you lean,
And sob most pitifully for all the lovely things that
    are not and have been.

"How silly I am!—and I *know* how silly I am!"
You say; "You are very patient. You are very kind.
I shall be better soon. Just Heaven consign and
    damn
To tedious Hell this body with its muddy feet in my
    mind!"

HUNTSMAN, WHAT QUARRY?

"HUNTSMAN, what quarry
On the dry hill
Do your hounds harry?

When the red oak is bare
And the white oak still
Rattles its leaves
In the cold air:
What fox runs there?"

"Girl, gathering acorns
In the cold autumn,
I hunt the hot pads
That ever run before,
I hunt the pointed mask
That makes no reply,
I hunt the red brush
Of remembered joy."

"To tame or to destroy?"

"To destroy."

"Huntsman, hard by
In a wood of grey beeches
Whose leaves are on the ground,
Is a house with a fire;
You can see the smoke from here.
There's supper and a soft bed
And not a soul around.
Come with me there;
Bide there with me;
And let the fox run free."

The horse that he rode on
Reached down its neck,
Blew upon the acorns,
Nuzzled them aside;
The sun was near setting;
He thought, "Shall I heed her?"
He thought, "Shall I take her
For a one-night's bride?"

He smelled the sweet smoke,
He looked the lady over;
Her hand was on his knee;
But like a flame from cover
The red fox broke—
And "Hoick! Hoick!" cried he.

PART FOUR

To Elinor Wylie
(Died 1928)

I

SONG FOR A LUTE

(1927)

SEEING how I love you utterly,
And your disdain is my despair,
Alter this dulcet eye, forbear
To wear those looks that latterly
You wore, and won me wholly, wear
A brow more dark, and bitterly
Berate my dulness and my care,
Seeing how your smile is my despair,
Seeing how I love you utterly.

Seeing how I love you utterly,
And your distress is my despair,
Alter this brimming eye, nor wear
The trembling lip that latterly
Under a more auspicious air
You wore, and thrust me through, forbear
To drop your head so bitterly

Into your hands, seeing how I dare
No tender touch upon your hair,
Knowing as I do how fitterly
You do reproach me than forbear,
Seeing how your tears are my despair,
Seeing how I love you utterly.

II

(1928)

For you there is no song . . .
   Only the shaking
Of the voice that meant to sing; the sound of the
     strong
   Voice breaking.

Strange in my hand appears
   The pen, and yours broken.
There are ink and tears on the page; only the tears
   Have spoken.

III

SONNET IN ANSWER TO A QUESTION
(1938)

Oh, she was beautiful in every part!—
The auburn hair that bound the subtle brain;
The lovely mouth cut clear by wit and pain,
Uttering oaths and nonsense, uttering art
In casual speech and curving at the smart
On startled ears of excellence too plain
For early morning!—*Obit*. Death from strain;
The soaring mind outstripped the tethered heart.

Yet here was one who had no need to die
To be remembered. Every word she said,
The lively malice of the hazel eye
Scanning the thumb-nail close—oh, dazzling dead,
How like a comet through the darkening sky
You raced! . . . would your return were heralded.

IV

NOBODY now throughout the pleasant day,
The flowers well tended and the friends not few,
Teases my mind as only you could do
To mortal combat erudite and gay . . .
"So Mr. S. was kind to Mr. K.!
Whilst Mr. K.—wait, I've a word or two!"
(I think that Keats and Shelley died with you—
They live on paper now, another way.)

You left in time, too soon; to leave too soon
Was tragic and in order—had the great
Not taught us how to die?—My simple blood,
Loving you early, lives to mourn you late . . .
As Mr. K., it may be, would have done;
As Mr. S. (*oh, answer!*) never would.

V

Gone over to the enemy now and marshalled against
   me
Is my best friend.

What hope have I to hold with my narrow back
This town, whence all surrender?

Someone within these walls has been in love with
     Death longer than I care to say;
It was not you! . . . but he gets in that way.

Gone under cover of darkness, leaving a running
    track,
And the mark of a dusty paw on all our splendour,
Are they that smote the table with the loudest blow,
Saying, "I will not have it so!"

No, no.
This is the end.
What hope have I?
You, too, led captive and without a cry!

VI

OVER THE HOLLOW LAND

OVER the hollow land the nightingale
Sang out in the full moonlight.
"Immortal bird,"
We said, who heard;
"What rapture, what serene despair;"
And paused between a question and reply
To hear his varied song across the tulip-scented air.

But I thought of the small brown bird among the
     rhododendrons at the garden's end,
Crouching, close to the bough,
Pale cheek wherefrom the black magnificent eye
     obliquely stared,
The great song boiling in the narrow throat
And the beak near splitting,
A small bird hunched and frail,
Whom the divine uncompromising note that brought
     the world to its window
Shook from head to tail.

Close to the branch, I thought, he cowers now,

Lest his own passion shake him from the bough.

Thinking of him, I thought of you . . .
Shaken from the bough, and the pure song half-way
through.

PART FIVE

THEME AND VARIATIONS

NOT even my pride will suffer much;
Not even my pride at all, maybe,
If this ill-timed, intemperate clutch
Be loosed by you and not by me,
Will suffer; I have been so true
A vestal to that only pride
Wet wood cannot extinguish, nor
Sand, nor its embers scattered, for,
See all these years, it has not died.

And if indeed, as I dare think,
You cannot push this patient flame,
By any breath your lungs could store,
Even for a moment to the floor
To crawl there, even for a moment crawl,
What can you mix for me to drink
That shall deflect me? What you do
Is either malice, crude defense
Of ego, or indifference:
I know these things as well as you;
You do not dazzle me at all.

Some love, and some simplicity,
Might well have been the death of me.

Heart, do not bruise the breast
That sheltered you so long;
Beat quietly, strange guest.

Or have I done you wrong
To feed you life so fast?
Why, no; digest this food
And thrive. You could outlast
Discomfort if you would.

You do not know for whom
These tears drip through my hands.
You thud in the bright room
Darkly. This pain demands
No action on your part,
Who never saw that face.

These eyes, that let him in,
(Not you, my guiltless heart)
These eyes, let them erase
His image, blot him out
With weeping, and go blind.

Heart, do not stain my skin
With bruises; go about
Your simple function. Mind,

Sleep now; do not intrude;
And do not spy; be kind.

Sweet blindness, now begin.

III

Rolled in the trough of thick desire,
No oars, and no sea-anchor out
To bring my bow into the pyre
Of sunset, suddenly chilling out
To shadow over sky and sea,
And the boat helpless in the trough;
No oil to pour; no power in me
To breast these waves, to shake them off:

I feel such pity for the poor,
Who take the fracas on the beam—
Being ill-equipped, being insecure—
Daily; and caulk the opening seam
With strips of shirt and scribbled rhyme;
Who bail disaster from the boat
With a pint can; and have no time,
Being so engrossed to keep afloat,
Even for quarrelling (that chagrined
And lavish comfort of the heart),
Who never came into the wind,
Who took life beam-on from the start.

And do you think that love itself,
Living in such an ugly house,
Can prosper long? We meet and part;
Our talk is all of heres and nows,
Our conduct likewise; in no act
Is any future, any past;
Under our sly, unspoken pact,
I know with whom I saw you last,
But I say nothing; and you know
At six-fifteen to whom I go.
Can even love be treated so?

I know, but I do not insist,
Having stealth and tact, though not enough,
What hour your eye is on your wrist.

No wild appeal, no mild rebuff
Deflates the hour, leaves the wine flat.

Yet if you drop the picked-up book
To intercept my clockward look—
Tell me, can love go on like that?

Even the bored, insulted heart,
That signed so long and tight a lease,
Can break its contract, slump in peace.

V

I had not thought so tame a thing
Could deal me this bold suffering.

I have loved badly, loved the great
Too soon, withdrawn my words too late;
And eaten in an echoing hall
Alone and from a chipped plate
The words that I withdrew too late.
Yet even so, when I recall
How ardently, ah! and to whom
Such praise was given, I am not sad:
The very rafters of this room
Are honoured by the guests it had.

You only, being unworthy quite
And specious,—never, as I think,
Having noticed how the gentry drink
Their poison, how administer
Silence to those they would inter—
Have brought me to dementia's brink.

Not that this blow be dealt to *me*:
But by thick hands, and clumsily.

Leap now into this quiet grave.
How cool it is. Can you endure
Packed men and their hot rivalries—
The plodding rich, the shiftless poor,
The bold inept, the weak secure—
Having smelt this grave, how cool it is?

Why, here's a house, why, here's a bed
For every lust that drops its head
In sleep, for vengeance gone to seed,
For the slashed vein that will not bleed,
The jibe unheard, the whip unfelt,
The mind confused, the smooth pelt
Of the breast, compassionate and brave.
Pour them into this quiet grave.

VII

Now from a stout and more imperious day
Let dead impatience arm me for the act.
We bear too much. Let the proud past gainsay
This tolerance. Now, upon the sleepy pact
That bound us two as lovers, now in the night
And ebb of love, let me with stealth proceed,
Catch the vow nodding, harden, feel no fright,
Bring forth the weapon sleekly, do the deed.

I know—and having seen, shall not deny—
This flag inverted keeps its colour still;
This moon in wane and scooped against the sky
Blazes in stern reproach. Stare back, my Will—
We can out-gaze it; can do better yet:
We can expunge it. I will not watch it set.

VIII

The time of year ennobles you.
The death of autumn draws you in.

The death of those delights I drew
From such a cramped and troubled source
Ennobles all, including you,
Involves you as a matter of course.

You are not, you have never been
(Nor did I ever hold you such),
Between your banks, that all but touch,
Fit subject for heroic song. . . .
The busy stream not over-strong,
The flood that any leaf could dam. . . .

Yet more than half of all I am
Lies drowned in shallow water here:
And you assume the time of year.

I do not say this love will last;
Yet Time's perverse, eccentric power
Has bound the hound and stag so fast
That strange companions mount the tower
Where Lockhart's fate with Keats is cast,
And Booth with Lincoln shares the hour.

That which has quelled me, lives with me,
Accomplice in catastrophe.

PART SIX

SONNET

Now that the west is washed of clouds and clear,
The sun gone under and his beams laid by,
You, that require a quarter of the sky
To shine alone in: prick the dusk, appear,
Beautiful Venus! The dense atmosphere
Cannot diffuse your rays, you blaze so high,
Lighting with loveliness a crisp and dry
Cold evening in the autumn of the year.

The pilot standing by his broken plane
In the unheard-of mountains, looks on you,
And warms his heart a moment at your light . . .
Benignant planet, sweet, familiar sight . . .
Thinking he may be found, he may again
See home, breaks the stale, buttered crust in two.

SONNET

BE SURE my coming was a sharp offense
And trouble to my mother in her bed;
And harsh to me must be my going hence,
Though I were old and spent and better dead;
Between the awful spears of birth and death
I run a grassy gauntlet in the sun;
And curdled in me is my central pith,
Remembering there is dying to be done.

O Life, my little day, at what a cost
Have you been purchased! What a bargain's here!
(And yet, thou canny Lender, thou hast lost:
Thumb thy fat book until my debt appear:
So . . . art thou stuck? . . . thou canst not strike that
    through
For the small dying that a man can do!)

SONNET

Enormous moon, that rise behind these hills
Heavy and yellow in a sky unstarred
And pale, your girth by purple fillets barred
Of drifting cloud, that as the cool sky fills
With planets and the brighter stars, distills
To thinnest vapour and floats valley-ward,—
You flood with radiance all this cluttered yard,
The sagging fence, the chipping window sills!

Grateful at heart as if for my delight
You rose, I watch you through a mist of tears,
Thinking how man, who gags upon despair,
Salting his hunger with the sweat of fright
Has fed on cold indifference all these years,
Praying God to make him worthy of such care.

SONNET

Now let the mouth of wailing for a time
Be shut, ye happy mourners; and return
To the marked door, the ribbon and the fern,
Without a tear. The good man in his prime,
The pretty child, the Gone—from a fair clime
Above the ashes of the solemn urn
Behold you; wherefore, then, these hearts that burn
With hot remorse, these cheeks the tears begrime?

Grief that is grief and worthy of that word
Is ours alone for whom no hope can be
That the loved eyes look down and understand.
Ye true believers, trusters in the Lord,
Today bereft, tomorrow hand in hand,
Think ye not shame to show your tears to me?

SONNET

I, too, beneath your moon, almighty Sex,
Go forth at nightfall crying like a cat,
Leaving the ivory tower I laboured at
For birds to foul and boys and girls to vex
With tittering chalk; and you, and the long necks
Of neighbours sitting where their mothers sat
Are well aware of shadowy this and that
In me, that's neither noble nor complex.

Such as I am, however, I have brought
To what it is, this tower; it is my own.
Though it was reared To Beauty, it was wrought
From what I had to build with: honest bone
Is there, and anguish; pride; and burning thought;
And lust is there, and nights not spent alone.

SONNET

WHEN did I ever deny, though this was fleeting,
That this was love? When did I ever, I say,
With iron thumb put out the eyes of day
In this cold world where charity lies bleating
Under a thorn, and none to give him greeting,
And all that lights endeavour on its way
Is the teased lamp of loving, the torn ray
Of the least kind, the most clandestine meeting?

As God's my judge, I do cry holy, holy,
Upon the name of love however brief,
For want of whose ill-trimmed, aspiring wick
More days than one I have gone forward slowly
In utter dark, scuffling the drifted leaf,
Tapping the road before me with a stick.

SONNET

Thou famished grave, I will not fill thee yet,
Roar though thou dost, I am too happy here;
Gnaw thine own sides, fast on; I have no fear
Of thy dark project, but my heart is set
On living—I have heroes to beget
Before I die; I will not come anear
Thy dismal jaws for many a splendid year;
Till I be old, I aim not to be eat.

I cannot starve thee out: I am thy prey
And thou shalt have me; but I dare defend
That I can stave thee off; and I dare say,
What with the life I lead, the force I spend,
I'll be but bones and jewels on that day,
And leave thee hungry even in the end.

SONNET

Upon this age, that never speaks its mind,
This furtive age, this age endowed with power
To wake the moon with footsteps, fit an oar
Into the rowlocks of the wind, and find
What swims before his prow, what swirls behind—
Upon this gifted age, in its dark hour,
Falls from the sky a meteoric shower
Of facts . . . they lie unquestioned, uncombined.

Wisdom enough to leech us of our ill
Is daily spun; but there exists no loom
To weave it into fabric; undefiled
Proceeds pure Science, and has her say; but still
Upon this world from the collective womb
Is spewed all day the red triumphant child.

SONNET

Count them unclean, these tears that turn no mill,
This salty flux of sorrow from the heart;
Count them unclean, and give me one day still
To weep, in an avoided room apart.
I shall come forth at length with reddened lid
Transparent, and thick mouth, and take the
  plough . . .
That other men may hope, as I once did;
That other men may weep, as I do now.

I am beside you, I am at your back
Firing our bridges, I am in your van;
I share your march, your hunger; all I lack
Is the strong song I cannot sing, you can.
You think we build a world; I think we leave
Only these tools, wherewith to strain and grieve.

SONNET

My earnestness, which might at first offend,
Forgive me, for the duty it implies:
I am the convoy to the cloudy end
Of a most bright and regal enterprise;
Which under angry constellations, ill-
Mounted and under-rationed and unspurred,
Set forth to find if any country still
Might do obeisance to an honest word.

Duped and delivered up to rascals; bound
And bleeding, and his mouth stuffed; on his knees;
Robbed and imprisoned; and adjudged unsound;
I have beheld my master, if you please.
Forgive my earnestness, who at his side
Received his swift instructions, till he died.